Stoyan Denchev
Irena Peteva

Global Political Crisis and Its Reflection on the Balkans

Stoyan Denchev
Irena Peteva

Global Political Crisis and Its Reflection on the Balkans

LAP LAMBERT Academic Publishing

Imprint

Any brand names and product names mentioned in this book are subject to trademark, brand or patent protection and are trademarks or registered trademarks of their respective holders. The use of brand names, product names, common names, trade names, product descriptions etc. even without a particular marking in this work is in no way to be construed to mean that such names may be regarded as unrestricted in respect of trademark and brand protection legislation and could thus be used by anyone.

Cover image: www.ingimage.com

Publisher:
LAP LAMBERT Academic Publishing
is a trademark of
Dodo Books Indian Ocean Ltd. and OmniScriptum S.R.L publishing group

120 High Road, East Finchley, London, N2 9ED, United Kingdom
Str. Armeneasca 28/1, office 1, Chisinau MD-2012, Republic of Moldova, Europe
Printed at: see last page
ISBN: 978-620-5-52819-8

Copyright © Stoyan Denchev, Irena Peteva
Copyright © 2022 Dodo Books Indian Ocean Ltd. and OmniScriptum S.R.L publishing group

CONTENTS

PREFACE 3

SUMMARY 7

INTRODUCTION 9

ECOLOGY AND NATURAL RESOURCES 11

ECONOMIC SANCTIONS AND TRADE WARS............................. 13

TRANSNATIONAL ORGANIZED CRIME AND THE INCREASING ACTIVITY OF GLOBAL NON-STATE PLAYERS 15

THE ROLE OF THE "LORDS" OF MODERN CYBERSPACE 17

DEMOGRAPHIC TRENDS AND MIGRATION 21

THE POLICIES OF THE UNATED STATES OF AMERICA, THE RUSSIAN FEDERATION, THE PEOPLE'S REPUBLIC OF CHINA, GREAT BRITAIN AND THE EUROPEAN UNION 23

INSTEAD OF CONCLUSION 29

AFTERWORDS 43

REFERENCES 47

This Scientific Study was supported by the National Scientific Program "Security & Defense";

Ministry of Education and Science of the Republic of Bulgaria, Agreement no. D01-74/19.05.2022.

PREFACE

AFTER DESCRIBING THE POLYCRISIS, THE NEXT STEP IS TO OVERCOME IT

Two renowned scientists (Irena Peteva and Stoyan Denchev) examine the "Global Political Crisis" and its "Impact on the Balkans" in their joint scientific study.

The Scientists Thomas Homer-Dixon, Ortwin Renn, Johan Rockstrom, Jonathan F. Donges and Scott Janzwood also agreed a year ago: "the world is not only plagued by an ever-increasing number of crises (economic and climate crisis, covid crisis and many more), these crises are also interconnected in a hardly transparent and hitherto unexplored way and thus one must speak of a major, global "polycrisis"".[1]

Irena Peteva and Stoyan Denchev probably see it that way, too, and analyse the "global crisis" (another word for the cited "polycrisis") on the basis of irreversible climate changes due to global warming, economic sanctions and trade wars, transnational organized crime, the upheavals caused by modern cyberspace, demographic trends and migration, the dominance claims of the USA, the Russian Federation and China, but also the interests of Great Britain and the European Union - here especially the lack of political coordination of the European Union - and examine the impact of this global crisis on the countries of the Balkans: Kosovo,

---

[1] Homer-Dixon, Thomas/Renn, Ortwin/Rockstrom, Johan/Donges, Jonathan F. and Janzwood, Scott: A Call for An International Research Program on the Risk of a Global Polycrisis (December 16, 2021). Available at SSRN: https://ssrn.com/abstract=4058592 or http://dx.doi.org/10.2139/ssrn.4058592

Serbia, Bulgaria, North Macedonia, Albania, Bosnia and Herzegovina and Montenegro.

One can read with great interest how this comprehensive analysis succeeds in just under 8,000 words and also very quickly understands the associated criticism of the perpetrators and actors of the named crises.

In the very readable analysis, one can also sense how the two Bulgarian scholars, with their love for their homeland - and for the Balkans as a whole - suffer from the polycrisis they describe and also make a connection between the cause and effect of the crises in the Balkan countries: "The Balkans are not only a kind of "consumer" of world political crises, but in some respects also their potential cause."

Therein also lies the great gain for me in reading this article.

The concept of the "global crisis" or the "polycrisis" in its overall impact on the countries of the Balkans cannot be understood if one does not assume that there is a mutual influence of the various fields of action and actors.

And knowing, identifying and being able to name this influence would probably be the first (albeit small) attempt to change something.

By the way, the authors very precisely and clearly point out the most important circumstance that can actually decrease the tension in the Balkans. And this is the full-right membership of the countries of the Western Balkans in the European Union (EU).

There are many objective opportunities and reasons for the EU to slow down this process referring to the formal obstacle of the impossibility for the membership conditions to be fulfilled.

It should be reminded that when "necessary", United Europe turned a blind eye and Bulgaria, Romania and Croatia received full accession to the EU without being fully prepared for that.

Another piece of evidence for the lack of principles in the EU policies is the situation in Sicily in Italy and Corsica in France. These two EU regions do not comply with the EU standards and directives. And so what – the EU exists anyway and is making attempts to develop.

In conclusion to their scientific study, Denchev and Peteva successfully suggest that regardless of the lack of sufficient preparation for EU membership, the Western Balkans countries can and definitely should be granted full-right membership to the European Union.

The proclaimed EU extension cannot be delayed indefinitely because the uncertainty of this process will enhance the negative impact of the global political crisis on the Balkans.

After describing the polycrisis, the next step is to want to overcome it, because we all don't want to hand over to our children a planet that is becoming increasingly less livable.

Prof. Dr. Martin Stieger,
Rector of Allensbach Hochschule,
Konstanz, Germany

SUMMARY

Today, peace in the world is being seriously tested. Without necessarily quoting Niccolò Machiavelli, it is not difficult to conclude that international security is currently almost at the height of monstrous and irreversible upheaval. Moving along the edge of their ill-fated outline, Homo Sapiens are "ready" once again to challenge the ancient Greek god of war – Ares and to disgrace his existence on planet Earth. And here we are not talking about the ubiquitous local conflicts (they have hardly stopped), but about a planned, as it were, large-scale planetary conspiracy to wipe out the human race. In whatever arbitrarily chosen direction we turn; in every corner of the world, we will always find the potential for sharp political opposition and the eventual outbreak of a military conflict. There are no longer any untouchable islands of long-term political stability on our planet. Everything is under imminence. Everything is threatened. And how long will this deadly game last? How long will mothers shed tears of grief and sorrow for their sons? How long will the insanity of the world's political, economic and military leaders dominate the sanity of billions of peaceful inhabitants on earth? How long...?

Questions ... without answers!

In the present analysis, we will try to give adequate answers to the posed questions on the scales of planetary chaos and we will project both the questions and the answers on a piece of land given by God to the peoples who have inhabited it for centuries. This blessed land is located in southeastern Europe and bears the flourishing name "the Balkans", after a legendary mountain (Stara Planina – Balkana), which crosses from end to end one of the most ancient countries in the world – Bulgaria.

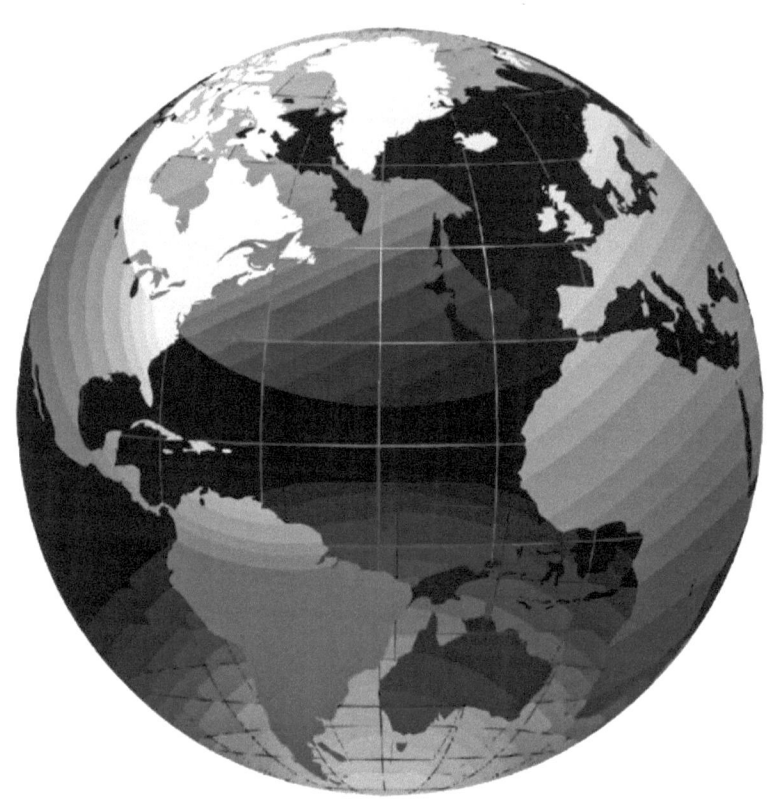

INTRODUCTION

Both in politics and in economy, at different periods of their development, there have always been dominant "players" in the world. By virtue of their economic and political power, they have been able to extend and impose their will on certain parts of the planet. At certain periods of human development, some of them even had claims to dominate the entire planet and this became a reality. In the short span of historical time of our present existence, almost nothing has changed. Such "players" still exist. Again, there are claims for dominance and hegemony. As the saying goes "there's nothing new under the sun".

After the end of the Second World War, a world order was established, which was soon after replaced by the so-called Cold War. The opposition of the two camps, led by the United States of America and the then Soviet Union, eventually succeeded in bringing about political, military, and economic parity in the world, which somehow unexpectedly collapsed with the collapse of the Soviet Union and the collapse of the countries of the so-called socialist camp. [1]

In this period, and to this day, we must not lose sight of the sharp fluctuations in the politics, the economy, and the culture of the Celestial Empire - China.

The developments in India and Pakistan had and continue to have a very strong influence not only on Asia but also on the whole world.

Latin America and Africa are the two sides of a planetary coin, as if minted for the purposes of global cash payments.

And where are the Balkans?

They are still in place and as always ready to ignite and burn in the flames of a new and irreversible military adventure.

ECOLOGY AND NATURAL RESOURCES

Irreversible climate changes associated with global warming have a huge impact on the health and lives of people all over the earth. Destructive hurricanes and floods, widespread droughts, and intense heat waves have a devastating effect on conscious human activity. Pollution of the natural environment, including vast expanses of water, leads to the endangerment of life on our planet. Uncontrolled urbanization is also a scourge of modern civilization.

And what are the measures? Almost none! Or if there are any, they are fragmentary and ineffective. The reckless exploitation of natural resources has led to their scarcity. It even went so far as to cut down nearly half of the world's available forest reserves. Globally, fresh water supplies are severely insufficient. Not to mention oil and its derivatives. Gas has become a tool of political violence.

As it has already been stated, the measures are almost none, and this is confirmed by the example of the current political leadership of the European Union. The so-called announced and forcibly imposed by this leadership "Green deal" is on the verge of a complete failure. Due to purely political and acute economic reasons, nuclear power plants were again put into regular operation on the territory of united Europe. Despite modern sewage treatment plants coal, gas and oil heating and power plants are once again poisoning the atmosphere with their dirty waste products.

Failure to deal with environmental problems is a symptom of a total global political crisis.

ECONOMIC SANCTIONS AND TRADE WARS

Trade wars are not yesterday's news. Although there are both global (WTO, WEF) and regional (EU, NAFTA, BRICS) trade organizations with declared regulatory functions, their influence on the main economic players is very limited.

The toolkit of economic sanctions has already become a kind of behavioural norm. The political, humanitarian and cultural cover of the sanctions cannot hide their expansionist nature. Through sanctions, those countries or unions try to force the rest of the world to work for them. The closure of existing transport corridors, the explosion of oil and gas pipelines (see "Nord Stream-2") is a vivid example of insurmountable not only political, but also economic contradictions on a global scale. It must be known that, on the other hand, sanctions are a "double-edged sword". It is not so much the large and economically powerful countries that suffer from them, but the ones that want to please their "elder brothers", and without having the necessary resources, out of infantilism and stupidity, and sometimes - due to compulsion - join the disorderly chorus of imitators.

Economic sanctions and trade wars are also characteristic symptoms of the total global political crisis.

TRANSNATIONAL ORGANIZED CRIME AND THE INCREASING ACTIVITY OF GLOBAL NON-STATE PLAYERS

Organized crime worldwide represents a vast, uncontrolled business empire that generates more than 7% of the world's gross domestic product (GDP). Recently, transnational criminal groups have penetrated more and more new territories by force and through bribery and occupy large market niches. Their activity is multifaceted. They are not limited to one or two economic sectors, but like insatiable spiders extend their networks for drug trafficking, money laundering, ammunition and arms trade, migrant trafficking, prostitution, trade in human organs, pedophilia, cultural values and in exotic animals. According to data from 2015-2020, the volume of "business" of these criminal syndicates reaches more than 5 trillion dollars.

The transnational organized crime network is in direct contact with many of the world's non-state actors. This relationship is expressed in the interpenetration of both their interests and their structures. When we talk about non-state players, we mean the following two branches:

First - those that represent the mimicry of certain intelligence, counterintelligence or military formations, created with the aim of concealing their true nature and their publicly unacceptable actions (see the so-called "Deep State");

Second – outright terrorist organizations such as al-Qaeda, Boco Haram, the Islamic state and al-Shabaab, which were created after the destruction of statehood in the Middle East (Syria, Yemen, Iraq) and north Africa (Libya). These terrorist organizations have neither the intention nor the ability to carry out even partially governmental functions in the field of domestic and foreign policy of the affected countries. Their only desire is to collect some funds in the form of taxes and fees and carry out public punitive actions against the population that does not agree with their policies.

After the failure and defeats suffered on the territory of the Middle East, some of the terrorist syndicates turned their attention to and established themselves permanently in Africa and Asia. The list of countries they have "infected" with their terrorist tactics is long, but it could start with Morocco, Somalia, Tunisia, Congo, Mozambique, Afghanistan and continue with Sri Lanka, Pakistan, and Malaysia. Their primary goal continues to be the erosion of statehood and the creation of instability in the world at large.

Transnational organized crime and global terrorist entities, with their pathologically distorted view of the world, are the "Achilles heel" of positive processes in the development of modern society.

THE ROLE OF THE "LORDS" OF MODERN CYBERSPACE

Information Civilization is another qualitative evolutionary stage in the development of social relations and social practices. It is characterized not only by the total dominance of information, but above all by cutting-edge technologies for its use in global social practice. [2]

At the basis of the emergence and development of the idea of Information Society as a new civilization model is change as the main driving force of social development. Modern change is determined by the importance of information as a basic resource for all spheres – politics, state administration, economy, education, health care, culture, etc. The process of changes covers the entire spectrum of social life, it is ubiquitous and irreversible. [3]

The main, distinctive features of Information Society can be reduced to a few, namely:

• democratic use of information resources - access to information is not only a legitimate right of citizens, but there are also technological possibilities for the majority of them to take advantage of this right.

• targeted search for information to make the most diverse decisions, including the most elementary ones, has become a mass need.

• absence of forceful censorship in both supply and access to information.

A basic principle of Information Society is that access to information is a basic human right, and information and communication technologies create prerequisites for its free use. Ultimately, the above unequivocally means that global information resources should be used democratically. [2] Is this so? The answer is - DEFINITELY NO!

When we talk about Information Civilization and Information Society, it is not only necessary, but also imperative to boldly enter their modern terminological paradigm. With certain approximations, the above can be summarized on the basis of a single term called **cyberspace**. According to the interpretive definition, given in Wikipedia, *"Cyberspace is a term that means the global network, as a set of independent information technology infrastructures, telecommunications networks, and computer systems in which online communication takes place."*

By Chip Morningstar and F. Randall Farmer, *The lessons of the Lucasfilm habitat. The new media reader*. Ed. Wardrip-Fruin and Nick Montfort: the MIT Press, 2003. 664-667.) „**cyberspace** is defined more by social interactions than by their technical implementation".

The well-known postulate of social development and social practice from the beginning of the 21st century states that whoever controls information controls the world. [4] Its modern interpretation can be summarized in the sentence that the lords of cyberspace are the masters of the world.

In this regard, it is logical to conclude that just as physical space needs protection, so cyberspace needs to be protected. [5] This implies that it should exist and develop in a specific security environment called cybersecurity. According to some regulatory documents, "cybersecurity is a state of society and the state in which, through the application of a complex of measures and actions, cyberspace is protected from threats related to its independent networks and information infrastructure or that may disrupt their work."[6]

We recently attended the launch of a university master's program with the sonorous and pretentious title of "Cybersecurity and Digital Forensics." The program was perfectly designed and brilliantly presented by its academic supervisor. At the beginning he said that whenever he hears the word cyberspace, he immediately associates it with the word cyberwar. We, for example, do not make such a connection. It is more natural for the term cyberspace to be associated, in the first place, with cyber ethics or, why not, with cyber diplomacy.

The control of cyberspace puts a key in the hands of its "masters" to effectively reduce or accelerate the global world political crisis. [7]

DEMOGRAPHIC TRENDS AND MIGRATION

In recent years there have been intensified and large-scale migration processes all over the world [8]. However, it is not precise to say that there are some demographic problems in the world. The correct wording here could be that recently there have been worsening demographic disproportions. At the expense of the growing population in India and China, in other regions of the world, a sharp decrease in human reproduction is observed. Not only certain countries, but entire regions are threatened by depopulation. In general, however, the population of the planet is increasing. At the moment, it is 8 billion, and it is expected to grow to 11 billion people by the end of this century. As we have already mentioned, from a geographical point of view this growth is uneven. It is also uneven in terms of age distribution. It has been observed that in developed countries the share of people at retirement age is increasing, while in poorer countries there is an increase in the proportion of young people.

The increasing number of people on our planet raises a number of questions, the most important of which are:

• is the world as a whole capable of providing conditions for a decent and dignified life for its citizens?

• does rapid population growth affect the environment?

• is access to the necessary natural resources, land for agricultural use, food and water ensured for all inhabitants of the earth?

Low living standards, frequent climatic upheavals, permanent changes in the environment, violence and conflicts lead to the migration of huge masses of the planet's population. This sometimes also results from the outright stupidity of the current political administration of individual countries or unions. It is with derision, much anger and undisguised regret, that we remember how a few years ago the political establishment of Germany, and of the European Union as well, issued an open invitation to people from the Middle East, Afghanistan and Central Asia to settle permanently in Europe. Apparently, they "did not count their chickens before they hatched" because the peoples of the European countries experienced this avalanche migration pressure as a huge disaster.

Statistics show that after 2020 and until now, a total of about 40 million people have migrated worldwide.

Large-scale migration processes, as well as worsening demographic disparities, are one of the clear symptoms of global political crisis.

THE POLICIES OF THE UNATED STATES OF AMERICA, THE RUSSIAN FEDERATION, THE PEOPLE'S REPUBLIC OF CHINA, GREAT BRITAIN AND THE EUROPEAN UNION

The United States of today continue to demonstrate to the world their understanding of their exceptional leadership in the attempts they make to impose their political-economic doctrine of the liberal agenda on humanity [9]. On the basis of their apparent superiority in the implementation of innovative technological solutions, they seek to erode existing international agreements in the field of non-proliferation of weapons of mass destruction and in the field of arms control. Under the administration of President Joe Biden, Washington is neither eager to conduct a constructive dialogue with the other "world players", nor to build bilateral and multilateral relations with them on the basis of mutual compromises and considering their primordial interests.

The Democratic party's dominance of the US Congress creates a base for the country's executive branch to consistently and methodically try to impose its neoliberal doctrine around the world. An important fact in the world political calendar were the so-called midterm elections, held in the USA in the first half of November this year. These elections are considered to be a test of sorts for the first half of President Joe Biden's administration. It is well-known that the US Congress consists of 210 representatives of the Republican party and 220 representatives of the Democratic party. In the Senate, the ratio is 48 democrats, 50 republicans and 2 independent senators. In this legislature, in the event of a tie, the vote of the Vice President, Ms. Kamala Harris, is pivotal.

The election in November showed not only to the citizens of America, but also to the world how Joe Biden's presidency has been evaluated and the result will greatly shape his behaviour for the rest of his term. If the representatives of the Republican party won both in the Congress and in the Senate, it would be extremely difficult for the President not only to push further his domestic policy, but his influence in the world would also be significantly reduced. However, the elections did not end according to general preliminary expectations. The big "red" wave didn't happen. It is true that the Republicans won the Congress, but the situation in the Senate remained the same. Although at this stage of development of the future political battle in the USA, the main opponent of President Biden is the former President Donald Trump, those who know the American political forest predict that a possible candidate of the Republican party for the next presidential elections will be the young, intelligent, moderate and assertive Ron DeSantis – current governor of the state of Florida

Political power in the Russian federation is concentrated in the hands of President Putin and his closest entourage. The Russian Duma is a kind of screen for Mr. Putin's policies, formulated and implemented on internal and external scale. We definitely want to emphasize that disregarding Russia's interests by the United States, Great Britain and the European union has led to the escalation of the tensions between Russia and Ukraine. President Putin's declared "Special Military Operation" has turned into a full-scale war, and many rightly believe that this war could evolve into World War III, where there will be no winners, and this will inevitably lead to the end of present day human civilization. In our opinion, regardless of the reasons for this war, there is no way we could justify the leadership of the Russian federation for the military actions they have undertaken. There is always an opportunity and it is necessary to look for peaceful solutions to the constantly arising political and economic contradictions in the world.

Recently, the Great British Empire lost one of world's longest reigning monarchs - Queen Elizabeth II. Her death naturally gave impetus to the development of a new political conjuncture in this country. Despite the negative expectations, King Charles III „showed character" at the very beginning of his reign and took a very authoritative stand as Head of State. The executive power, though, is in a process of temporary turmoil, which is already in the process of subsiding. The failed election of Mrs. Liz Trust as Prime Minister of the United Kingdom caused a lot of damage to the English political system. However, with the election of Mr. Rishi Sunak to this position, the expectations are that this will be overcome.

Since leaving the European Union, Britain has been trying to play its game on the world political stage and, so far, that game is going well. With strong support from the USA, Britain is seeking to push the European Union out of its traditional spheres of global influence and at the present moment it is succeeding.

China has always been and still is a mystery to the rest of the world. Since the beginning of the century this country, which still has the most numerous population in the world, has occupied the leading position in global economy. Even the smallest device, created anywhere in the world, contains at least one component made in China. This applies with particular force in the field of modern information and communication technologies. One of the main hallmarks of the foreign policy, led by the Celestial Empire, is the One China principle (for now, in two countries - mainland

China and Taiwan). The demonstrative and unwelcome visit of US House Speaker Nancy Pelosi to Taiwan showed China's determination to protect its interests by all means.

Despite not showing visible support for Russia in the war in Ukraine, China, through its apparent neutrality and economic aid to Russia, shows whose interests it is protecting.

Recently, the most important political and economic forum of the Chinese state was held - another congress of the Chinese Communist Party. This congress confirmed China's current development course and strengthened the place and role of the President of this country and Chairman of the Chinese Communist Party, Mr. Xi Jinping.

Against the background of the role, place and importance of the USA, Russia, Great Britain and the PR of China on the world political stage, the European Union is gradually becoming a political dwarf, an appendage of its largest overseas partner. The latest 'edition' of the political establishment of united Europe shows visible infantilism. Lack of clear vision for the development of the Union, highly bureaucratized management system and blind pursuit of foreign political goals definitely lead the European union to a dead end. Parting ways with traditional European Christian values has caused and continues to cause irreparable damage to European social development.

In order to take its rightful place on the global world economic and political stage, a united Europe needs large-scale and urgent changes. Changes that fundamentally revise not only the so-called executive body of the Union - the European Commission, but also its so-called legislative body – the European Parliament.

Lack of synchronization in the policies of the USA, Russia, Great Britain, China and the European Union is visible everywhere, a major symptom of a total global political crisis.

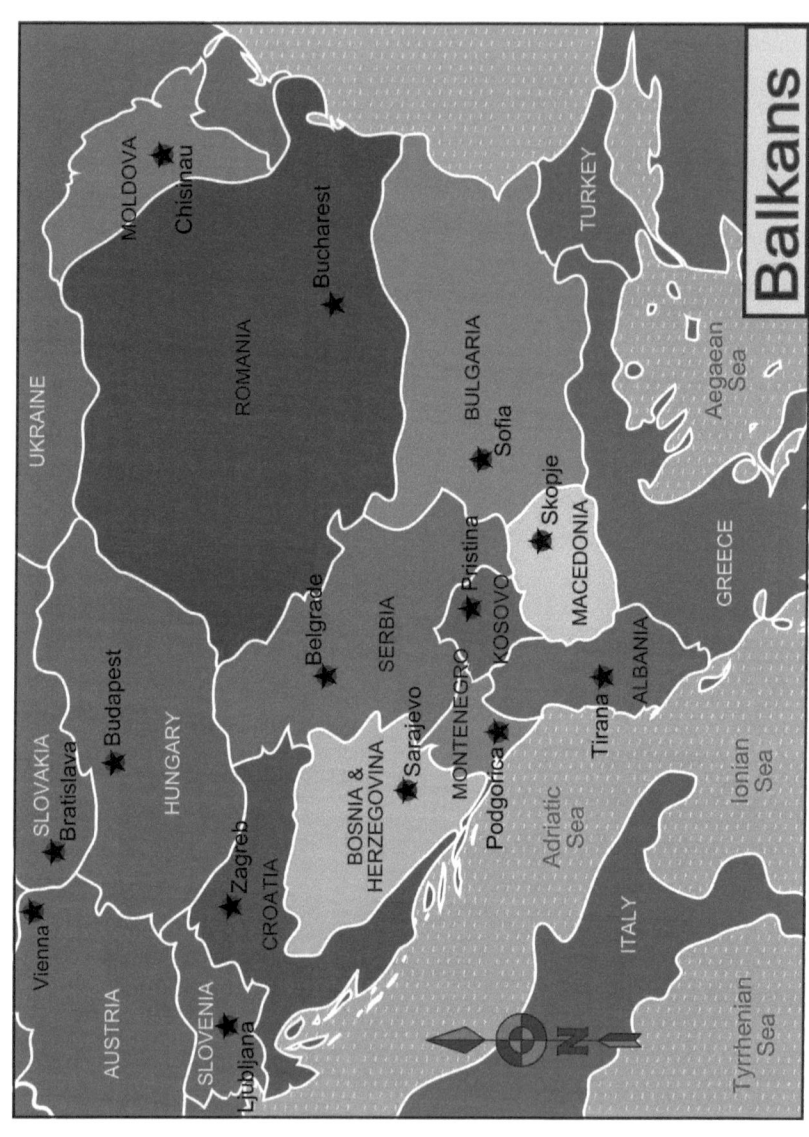

Map Author: Peter Fitzgerald

INSTEAD OF CONCLUSION

The summarizing paradigmatic synthesis of the discussed topic has not only a direct relationship with the current state of world civilization development, but its influence also has a highly destructive character.

For researchers of world political processes, for serious political observers, players and connoisseurs, one of the peculiar litmus tests of modern geopolitics is the current and reliably predictable situation on the Balkans. At this point, we would not like to quote thoughts, conclusions and generalizations, expressed by political shamans, "strangers" to the region. However, it seems that in the end these so-called thoughts could be summed up by the long-known statement that "the Balkans are a powder keg". Careless attitude and ill-intentioned political and economic treatment of the countries of the Balkan Peninsula can cause irreparable damage not only to the Old continent, but also to the whole world.

The above-mentioned main characteristic features of the growing world political (and economic) crisis, such as:

- insurmountable environmental problems;
- economic sanctions and trade wars;
- lack of real ethical dimensions in cyberspace;
- destructive demographic trends and uncontrolled migration;
- transnational organized crime;
- increasing activity of global non-state entities;

• specifics and non-constructive role of the main world political players – the USA, Russia, China, Great Britain and the European Union,

have a strong and hard-to-overcome influence on the political and economic situation on the Balkans.

Taking into account the fact that both countries are members of NATO, Turkiye and Greece are in permanently strained relations. Of course, these relations have historical roots, too, but they became particularly acute after the Turkish occupation of Northern Cyprus and the establishment of the Turkish Republic of Northern Cyprus (Turkish Federated State of Cyprus). Recently, we have witnessed a renewed acrimony in Greek-Turkish relations based on their disputes over oil and gas exploration in the Mediterranean.

Some of the nuances of the world political crisis are also at the basis of the permanent tension between Serbia and the newly self-declared state of the Republic of Kosovo. The confrontation has not stopped there and will not stop anytime soon. Today's Serbia does not recognize Kosovo and, ignoring the realities, still continues to treat this country as the Former Yugoslav Republic. The ongoing dispute over car registration plates, as well as the one over the legitimacy of identity documents for citizens of the Republic of Kosovo of Serbian origin, are just another episode in the still simmering and intractable conflict between Serbs and Kosovars. If the so-called great world powers have not reached even a formal agreement to reduce the tension in this part of the Balkans, this conflict has the real potential to grow and become not only European, but also global. When analyzing the situation in and around Kosovo, the fact is that on the territory of this country, on its border with North Macedonia, the largest US military base in Europe is located - Camp-Bondsteel, with a staff of between 7,000 and 25,000 people.

The current events in northern Kosovo are reminiscent of the events during the last decade of the 20th century. Everyone is clearly aware that the present-day situation is not beneficial to anyone. Recently, under the auspices of the European Commission, a kind of negotiation marathon began between the President of Serbia, Mr. Aleksandar Vucic, and the Prime Minister of Kosovo, Mr. Albin Kurti, to get out of the painful confrontational situation. The US State Department indirectly intervened in this marathon, urging the two countries to make the necessary efforts for a fair compromise in order to guarantee the fragile peace in the region. In addition, the US State Department called on the authorities in Kosovo to stop any planned measures that could directly escalate tensions in this republic, which is not recognized by Serbia. The President of Serbia, Mr. Vucic, emotionally asked the Kosovo Serbs to keep the peace by making the necessary compromises so as not to be blamed for their unconstructive behaviour. Many vicissitudes and difficulties had been overcome and, in the end, Mr. Josep Borrell, High Representative of the European Union for Foreign Affairs and Security Policy, declared that an agreement had been reached between Belgrade and Pristina.

This fact is of significant importance, because preserving the peace between Kosovo and Serbia is an irrevocable imperative!

The political sway from one extreme to another in the selection and in the servility to "Big Brother" is a characteristic feature of Bulgarian political system. From the most faithful friend and ally of the former Soviet Union, Bulgaria "transferred" its boundless devotion and love to the Western European and Transatlantic political systems. Embracing the so-called Euro-Atlantic values, Bulgarian politicians left the original Bulgarian values at the background. On the other hand, it is quite normal for Bulgaria, being a member of the European Union and NATO, to be part of the so-called democratic world and to actively recognize its values. However, there is a well-known Bulgarian proverb that goes - "It's too much of a good thing". The expected but very rapid repainting of quite a few leading political figures in Bulgaria puts off from politics a large part of the population of the country, and this is evident from the large number of non-voters in the series of snap parliamentary elections. The political landscape in Bulgaria is very unstable. The only "anchor" in this turbulent political environment is the President of the Republic, directly elected by the people.

If you ignore the formally strained relations with the Republic of North Macedonia, Bulgaria has wonderful, mutually beneficial relations with its neighbours on the Balkans.

Declaring its desire for membership in the European union, the Republic of North Macedonia is still far from its practical realization. Certainly, it is very important for the citizens of this country to be citizens of united Europe, but it seems that the desire of certain Euro-Atlantic external powers for such membership dominates the political life of Macedonia. Until recently, some analysts pointed out the destructive role of the Russian Federation in the process of joining North Macedonia to the European Union, but even if there were such attempts, they are no longer relevant. The role of a negative political avatar in this process currently "falls" to Serbia, as an outpost of Russia in the Balkans.

Assuming the following circumstances that (1) all Bulgarians believe that Macedonians are Bulgarians (and this is the historical truth); and that (2) not only constitutionally, but also de facto, North Macedonia is a multinational state with parity between Macedonians and Albanians, and (3) if there are insurmountable obstacles to the acceptance of North Macedonia into united Europe or this process is delayed too long, there is a real danger of strong ethnic opposition in this country, which has the potential to escalate into civil war.

Before the global social changes at the end of the twentieth century, Albania was barely visible on the world political stage. Isolated from both the West and the East, for decades, under the leadership of its party leader Enver Hoxha, this impoverished Balkan state was of no visible interest to global political players. After the successful attempts to democratize the Albanian political system, interest in it is now noticeable. When we talk about attempts, we mean that the political processes in Albania are quite turbulent and unstable. The long reign of Mr. Sali Berisha, as President and as Prime Minister and the subsequent reigns of his political opponents have sharpened the political opposition in this country to the extreme. The Albanian citizens got some relative peace during the time when their President was the moderate politician Mr. Ilir Meta. Due to the eccentric nature and irrelevant statements of the current Prime Minister of Albania, Mr. Edi Rama, and the deepening economic problems of the country, it is quite possible that in the foreseeable future, the Albanian voters will give power back to the former President Ilir Meta.

Quite a few of the so-called great powers react extremely sharply to the fact that the Albanian political elite considers unification with Kosovo and the Albanians in North Macedonia to be its strategic goal. And here the problem is not even in the fact that Kosovo (not only according to Serbia, but also according to Russia) is still part of Serbia. Due to complex internal contradictions, this idea is also strongly supported by one NATO country - Spain. Regardless of the publicly declared support for Kosovo, many NATO countries consider Albanian nationalism particularly destructive, because the possible realization of this idea would open "Pandora's box".

It is a well-known fact that on the Balkans each nation has its own concept of a "Great Motherland", which necessarily includes large territories of its neighbours. All these concepts are dangerous, but two of them are treated as the most disturbing and destructive - the concept of Greater Albania and that of Greater Serbia.

The newly formed state of Bosnia and Herzegovina was one of the six federal entities that made up the former Socialist Federal Republic of Yugoslavia (SFRY). Bosnia and Herzegovina won its independence in the 1990s (March 3rd, 1992), during the wars in former Yugoslavia. In accordance with the so-called Dayton Agreement (December 14th, 1995) this country is a Protectorate, administered by a High Representative elected by the Parliament of the European Union. [10] Administratively, the country is divided into two parts and one district: Federation of Bosnia and Herzegovina, Respublika Srpska and Brčko district.

In 2013, a population census was conducted in Bosnia and Herzegovina, which showed the following results: the total population was 3,531,159 people. According to ethnic traditions and political realities on this territory of the Balkans, the three official "state-defining" peoples are: Bosnians - about 50%, Serbs - about 31%, Croats - about 15% and others - about 4%). Religious affiliation of the three relatively large minority groups is as follows - Muslims - 51%, Orthodox Christians - 30.7% and Catholics - 15.2%.

The influential political parties in Bosnia and Herzegovina are ethnically based and they are: Union of Independent Social Democrats (primarily based on the Serb ethnic community), Croatian Democratic Community of Bosnia and Herzegovina (primarily composed on the basis of the Croat ethnic community) and Party of Democratic Action (consisting primarily of the Bosniak ethnic community).

At this point we would like to draw attention to the most important thing that threatens the fragile unity of this multinational state, which is that both Bosnian Serbs and Bosnian Croats have a strategic goal to separate from the state of Bosnia and Herzegovina and join respectively Serbia and Croatia. And here the threats are real. The parties of Mr. Milorad Dodik and Mr. Dragan Covic are actively cooperating in the increasingly radical dismemberment of Bosnia and Herzegovina. Attacks against the state also have a second plan. Among other things, Covic calls for a new territorial reorganization of the country. He argued that Croats were underrepresented and his goal was to create a third, Croat-dominated administrative structure. The unity of this country is also threatened by the denial of the Srebrenica genocide by both Croatian and Serbian extremists.

In its previous meetings, the European Commission unanimously recommended to the "summit meeting" in December 2022 that the Council of the European Union grant Bosnia and Herzegovina the status of a candidate for membership in the European Union because, in the light of the Ukrainian crisis and in the name of peace and stability of the Western Balkans, it is of historical importance for Bosnia and Herzegovina to acquire this status.

Due to the same reasons, at the last summit of the European Union, such status was awarded to both Ukraine and Moldova. In this regard and as a confirmation of the good intentions of united Europe, the newly elected member of the Presidency of Bosnia and Herzegovina, Mr. Denis Bećirović, made the following encouraging statement at the inauguration: "My vision for Bosnia and Herzegovina is a European Bosnia and Herzegovina and the development of common identity. Let's strengthen the security of Bosnia and Herzegovina, because we know first-hand that peace and economic development require all of us, while a conflict does not. Politicians in Bosnia and Herzegovina should not be selfish and work in their own interest. We should work in the interest of poor people. We should not sow hatred in order to be popular... Let's increase cooperation with friendly countries. Regional cooperation with neighbouring countries is also important for peace, stability, establishing trade relations and cultural cooperation."

It is a pity that official Brussels is also used in the intervention in the affairs of Bosnia and Herzegovina. Croatia, as a member of the European Union, uses all European institutions to oppose democratic reforms in that country and advocates for more special rights for the Croatian community.

Montenegro gained its independence through a referendum held on May 21st, 2006. On June 3rd of the same year, the Montenegrin Parliament officially announced the country's independence, and on September 10th the first parliamentary elections were held after the declaration of the country's independence. The so-called coalition "for a European Montenegro", composed of the Democratic party of socialists, headed by Mr. Milo Djukanović and the Social democratic party, headed by Mr. Ranko Krivokapić, got 41 seats in the new 81-members Parliament and secured the necessary majority in the country's legislative body. On the basis of this victory, Mr. Krivokapic was elected as the Speaker of the Assembly, and Mr. Djukanovic - as the Prime Minister of the country.

The current government in Montenegro reports a decent economic boom, largely due to successful tourism seasons in the pandemic year and beyond/the years that followed. According to official data, the tourism sector forms more than a quarter of the country's gross domestic product (GDP). An interesting fact in the tourism industry was that tourists from Ukraine outnumbered tourists from Russia. It should not be forgotten that in 2019 Montenegro was declared the Fastest growing tourist destination in Europe. On the other hand, however, the National air carrier of Montenegro went bankrupt. The one-billion-dollar contract signed with the "export-import" Bank of China, with the aim of "China Road & Bridge Corporation" to build a modern highway between the largest sea port of Montenegro - the city of Bar and the city of Belgrade - the capital of Serbia, also failed. According to the plan, this highway should be 435 km long, with 40 bridges and 90 tunnels. Considering all the pros and cons of this large-scale construction, all world experts agree that the highway has become a threat to the country's economic stability. And as the New York times notes: "The highway is one of the most expensive road infrastructures in the world, and because of this, Montenegro is saddled with debts to China that amount to more than a third of its annual budget."

Perhaps unexpectedly for many, Montenegro took a big step in its rapprochement with the West, becoming the 29th member of NATO, although until then its relations with the Russian Federation were excellent. These ties are based not only on diplomatic or economic logic, but also on the historical and religious proximity between the two countries. Montenegro's membership in the North Atlantic Treaty Organization has strained its relationship with Moscow, which in turn represents part of the global political crisis and a potential local source of tension.

And one more thing - in 2020, the acting Metropolitan of the Serbian orthodox church and its deputy in Montenegro died suddenly. As a follow-up of these events, in the autumn of 2022 the country again became the centre of crisis on the Balkans. The reason for this crisis was the ordination, by the Serbian orthodox church, of the clergyman Joanikije II as Metropolitan of Montenegro.

Many global as well as local initiatives are permanently generated on the Balkans. These initiatives involve various countries in the region whose strategic goal is, at the end of the day, membership in the European Union and the North Atlantic Alliance.

During Bulgaria's Presidency of the Council of the European Union (from January 1st to June 30th 2018), the issue of the accession of the Balkan countries to united Europe was raised once again with great intensity. On this basis, the so-called regional initiative, The Berlin Process, received a big boost again, which radically changed the approach to the integration of Western Balkan countries into the European Union. This initiative was launched in 2014 by the Federal Republic and the United Kingdom.

The Berlin process started just when euroscepticism was at its peak. This process aimed to revive the multilateral relations between Balkan countries and the member states of the European Union. Its sub-goals covered both the improvement of regional cooperation between the Balkan countries in the field of their economic development and the awakening of the "sleeping European conscience" for the expected enlargement of the European Union.

The Open Balkan (Mini-Schengen) initiative is a unique regional initiative. The beginning of this initiative was set in October 2019 in the city of Novi Sad, Serbia, at a meeting between the President of that country, Mr. Aleksandar Vucic, and the Prime Ministers of Albania and North Macedonia, Mr. Edi Rama and Mr. Zoran Zaev. In addition to the founding countries, Montenegro and Bosnia and Herzegovina also participate in some summits, but have not yet received the status of full members of the initiative.

In addition, the United States, in support of the Open Balkan initiative, launched the so-called Washington agreement of September 2020 between Serbia and Kosovo, which envisages that Kosovo will also join the Open Balkan, but unfortunately this has not happened yet.

Open Balkan is a working idea for an accelerated technology for the countries of the Western Balkans to restore trust among themselves more quickly and prepare for membership in united Europe faster. As a result of this initiative, they should create effective prerequisites for a unified approach to the European Union, as a group of countries with clearly defined goals and interests.

A reasonable assumption can definitely be made that in the Berlin process and in the Open Balkan initiative natural compatibility has consciously been sought, since both have a clear goal - real membership of the participating countries in the European Union, by building a stronger political, economic and cultural form of cooperation among themselves.

While the so-called Berlin process is primarily a kind of mechanism to achieve the German and in particular the British interests on the Balkans, the Open Balkan initiative is a specific idea of some of the leaders in the region who sincerely wish to restore lost trust among themselves and to launch new forms of future cooperation among the countries they lead [11].

Regardless of the mentioned initiatives, the Balkans still remain an area of political turbulence, uncertainty and instability.

In any case, the uncertainty and instability of this ancient land will present the European Union with intractable challenges. United Europe will find predicaments in its intentions to establish a long-term strategic position in global political and economic relations and to respond to the challenges of globalization.

Europe needs to demonstrate vision regarding its enlargement. As a rule, the countries of the European Union are always tempted to impose various unenforceable membership conditions on potential candidates. Nevertheless, they should refrain from such "artificial" blockades and seek solutions to such problems. Otherwise, countries like China and Russia will constantly try to strengthen their influence on the Balkans, and under their permanent pressure some Balkan countries may change their "fragile" geopolitical orientation.

Balkans, Balkans, ancient land of ancient nations. There are many countries in this corner of Paradise and there are twice as many problems that they independently or with foreign "help" generate.

The Balkans are not only a kind of "consumer" of world political crises, but in certain respects they are also their potential generator.

It's a pity, but a fact!

AFTERWORDS

THE AUTHORS HIGHLIGHT THE MOST IMPORTANT CHARACTERISTICS IN THE CHANGING WORLD ...

"Global Political Crisis and its Impact on the Balkans" is a scientific study that presents a timely and accurate analysis of the changing geopolitical environment.

The United Nations, established after the Second World War, defined the conditions for not allowing the "God of War" (as the authors aptly put it) to rule human affairs. Over decades of bipolar ideological, military and economic opposition it seemed that this goal had been achieved thanks to the implementation of cutting-edge scientific and technical achievements and technologies in military affairs, which turned the thesis of "continuation of policy by other means" into a shortcut to mutual destruction.

The end of Cold war, in fact, gave us the opportunity for a civilized assessment and understanding that the security we pursued with military technologies is actually part of the essence of the concept of security. In order to be able to ensure the existence of our civilization, we need to build a society with functional areas that give us the opportunity for development - individual, public, national, civilized.

It is these functional areas in particular that have been explored by the authors, and each of them can be the subject of a separate analysis. And regardless of the expectations for the decline of "war" as a political instrument of violence, the authors highlight the most important characteristics in the changing world - violence covers all functional areas of our lives: ecology, economy, trade, digitization, which turn into "economic sanctions", "trade wars", "cyber wars".

Attention is paid to "cyber space", which, on the one hand, is the catalyst that has unlocked the turbulent globalization processes, and on the other, is the achievement of civilization that makes us both strong and weak at the same time. The analyses would not be complete if the importance of the nucleus (core) in the system of functional areas of society and civilization was not considered - demography with its trends.

After the analysis of the problems in the construction of the functional areas of security or, as it is customary to call it, "peaceful" development, the authors consider the influence of the leading countries, who we also call front-runners of leading economies and global processes.

The analysis based on examples, given by the authors, confirms the necessary conclusions for minimizing the role of the UN and following the established international norms in relations as well as imposing the concept of "world order based on rules", which, however, are defined by the "West" in their role as a global economic and military power. It is this contradiction on a global scale that also raises questions about the established mechanisms and tools for our civilized development. It is in these mechanisms and tools that the authors see reasons for the processes that are evolving on the Balkans such as a "political sway from one extreme to another", leaving national values in the background, proclaiming Euro-Atlantic values as the only significant ones. In this way, according to the authors, nationalistic unaccomplished national aspirations awaken and new risks are created.

The scientific study, compiled by Prof. Denchev and Prof. Peteva, reaffirms the capacity of the University of Library Studies and Information Technology, Sofia, Bulgaria to nurture abilities for a multifaceted analysis of events in their students, who have realized their purpose in life.

Hon. Prof. Emil Lyutskanov, PhD,

Vice Admiral (Res.)

REFERENCES

[1] S. **Denchev**, S. **Yordanova**. The Biological Weapon as a Tool for Psychological Impact in the Context of Hybrid Warfare. In: Journal of Social and Political Sciences, Vol.3, 2020, pp. 875 – 882. ISSN 2615-3718.

[2] **Denchev**, S., Informatsia i sigurnost, Akademichno izdatelstvo „Za Bukvite – O pismenehy", ISBN:978- 619-185-369-4, Sofia, 2019

[**Денчев**, С., Информация и сигурност, Академично издателство „За Буквите – О писменехь", ISBN:978- 619-185-369-4, София, 2019]

[3] **Peteva**, I., **Denchev** S., CULTURE DE TRANSPARENCE, Société, information, bibliothèques, Préface de Robert Estivals, L'Harmattan, France, 2010, ISBN : 978-2-296-13060-9

[4] **Denchev**, S. **Stoeva**, D. Kiberdiplomatsiyata – neobhodimata nova podredba na starite politicheski bardatsi. V: sp. Natsionalna sigurnost. s. 27 broy 10/2022. ISSN: 2682-941X & ISSN: 2682-9983.

[**Денчев**, С. **Стоева**, Д. Кибердипломацията – необходимата нова подредба на старите политически бардаци. В: сп. Национална сигурност. с. 27 брой 10/2022. ISSN: 2682-941X & ISSN: 2682-9983.]

[5] **Bosakova**, Kristina. Bazovi aspekti na kibersigurnostta. Studia. Sofia, 2019. 48 s. ISBN 978-619-185-374-8

[**Босакова**, Кристина. Базови аспекти на киберсигурността. Студия. София, 2019. 48 с. ISBN 978-619-185-374-8]

[6] Закон за кибесигурност, Обн. ДВ. бр.94 от 13 Ноември 2018г., изм. ДВ. бр.69 от 4 Август 2020г., изм. и доп. ДВ. бр.85 от 2 Октомври 2020г., изм. и доп. ДВ. бр.15 от 22 Февруари 2022г., изм. ДВ. бр.25 от 29 Март 2022г., Lex.bg

[7] **Yotova**, R. „Inteligentnata informatsia" – strategicheski instrument za garantirane na sigurnostta v usloviyata na savremennia informatsionen svyat. - V: Sbornik s dokladi ot Godishna universitetska nauchna konferentsia, 30 yuni - 1 yuli 2022, Veliko Tarnovo. Veliko Tarnovo: NVU "Vasil Levski", 2022, s. 263 - 273. ISSN 1314-1937

[**Йотова**, Р. „Интелигентната информация" – стратегически инструмент за гарантиране на сигурността в условията на съвременния информационен свят. - В: Сборник с доклади от Годишна университетска научна конференция, 30 юни - 1 юли 2022, Велико Търново. Велико Търново: НВУ "Васил Левски", 2022, с. 263 - 273. ISSN 1314-1937]

[8] **Yordanova**, S. Analiz na aktualnata globalna politiko-ikonomicheska informatsionna sreda. – V: Obshtestvoto na znanieto i humanizmat na HHI vek. Sofia: Za bukvite – O pismenehy, 2021, s. 511 – 520, ISSN 2683-0094

[**Йорданова**, С. Анализ на актуалната глобална политико-икономическа информационна среда. – В: Обществото на знанието и хуманизмът на XXI век. София: За буквите – О писменехь, 2021, с. 511 – 520, ISSN 2683-0094]

[9] **Plotnikov**, N., Svetat na raba na planetarnia haos, Spisanie „Geopolitika & Geostrategia, broy 4, 2021, str.111, ISSN 1312-4579

[**Плотников**, Н., Светът на ръба на планетарния хаос, Списание „Геополитика & Геостратегия, брой 4, 2021, стр.111, ISSN 1312-4579]

[10] **Todorov**, A., Izcherpani li sa vazmozhnostite na Bosnenskia protektorat, Spisanie „Geopolitika & Geostrategia, broy 4, 2021, str.15, ISSN 1312-4579

[**Тодоров**, А., Изчерпани ли са възможностите на Босненския протекторат, Списание „Геополитика & Геостратегия, брой 4, 2021, стр.15, ISSN 1312-4579]

[11] **The "mini-Schengen"** regional cooperation initiative launched on 10 October 2019 in Novi Sad included Serbia, North Macedonia and Albania. The initiative was renamed into "Open Balkan" on 29 July 2021 at a meeting in Skopje. It is expected that Bosnia and Herzegovina, Montenegro and Kosovo will also join the initiative.

I want morebooks!

Buy your books fast and straightforward online - at one of world's fastest growing online book stores! Environmentally sound due to Print-on-Demand technologies.

Buy your books online at
www.morebooks.shop

Kaufen Sie Ihre Bücher schnell und unkompliziert online – auf einer der am schnellsten wachsenden Buchhandelsplattformen weltweit! Dank Print-On-Demand umwelt- und ressourcenschonend produziert.

Bücher schneller online kaufen
www.morebooks.shop

 info@omniscriptum.com
www.omniscriptum.com

Printed by Books on Demand GmbH, Norderstedt / Germany